This edition copyright © 2001 Lion Publishing
Illustrations copyright © 2001 Danuta Mayer
Published by
Lion Publishing plc
Sandy Lane West, Oxford, England
www.lion-publishing.co.uk
ISBN 0 7459 4758 1
First edition 2001
10 9 8 7 6 5 4 3 2 1 0
All rights reserved

Acknowledgments

16: from 'Disclosure' in *Candles and Kingfishers* © 1993, 1997 Foundery Press. Used by permission of Methodist Publishing House. 22, 23, 25, 26, 28, 45, 49: from the *Holy Bible, New International Version*, copyright © 1973, 1978, 1984 by International Bible Society. Used by permission. 24, 27, 32, 35, 42, 61: from the Good News Bible published by The Bible Societies/HarperCollins Publishers Ltd, UK © American Bible Society 1966, 1971, 1976, 1992, used with permission. 38: from *The 'Times' Book of Prayers*, Mowbray, copyright © 1997 David Gray. Used by permission.

A catalogue record for this book is available from the British Library

Typeset in Throhand Regular
Printed and bound in China

Pause
for a moment

Prayers
for busy people

Compiled by Rebecca Winter

Illustrated by Danuta Mayer

Introduction

It is an old custom of the servants of God to have some little prayers ready to hand, and to be frequently darting them up to heaven during the day.

ST PHILIP NERI

May this book of
short prayers be
a ready-to-hand
quiver of 'arrows'
to be shot straight
from the heart to
a listening God.

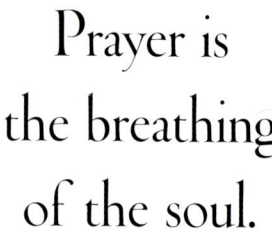

Prayer is the breathing of the soul.

ST JOHN OF KRONSTADT

Prayer is the holy water that by its flow makes the plants of our good desires grow green and flourish.

ST JOHN VIANNEY

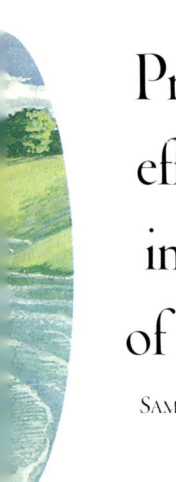

Prayer is the effort to live in the spirit of the whole.

SAMUEL TAYLOR COLERIDGE

Prayer is
a state of
continual
gratitude.

St John of Kronstadt

Prayer is an exercise of the spirit, as thought is of the mind.

MARY F. SMITH

Prayer is
God
being God
in me
being me.

Tom Wright

Prayer is like watching for the kingfisher.

All you can do
is be where he is
likely to appear,
and wait.

ANN LEWIN

Day by day,
dear Lord,
three things
I pray:

To see thee more
clearly,
Love thee more
dearly,
Follow thee more
nearly,
Day by day.

St Richard of Chichester

Sunday

*Be still,
and know that
I am God.*

Psalm 46:10

Help me to be still.
Help me to know
that you are God.

Monday

*This is the day
the Lord has made;
let us rejoice
and be glad in it.*

Psalm 118:24

I will be glad,
whatever the day holds.

Tuesday

My saving power will rise on you like the sun.

MALACHI 4:2

May the sunshine of your power and love shine within me.

Wednesday

As a mother comforts her child, so will I comfort you.

Isaiah 66:13

Thank you, God.

Thursday

You will seek me and find me when you seek me with all your heart.

Jeremiah 29:13

I seek you, God; my heart is open.

Friday

*You will have peace
by being united to me.*

John 16:33

And in that unity
may I bring peace
to others.

Saturday

What does the Lord require of you? To act justly and to love mercy and to walk humbly with your God.

Micah 6:8

May justice,
mercy and humility
govern my thoughts
and actions today
and every day.

When you pray, I will answer you.

ISAIAH 58:9

The things
I pray for, give
me the grace
to work for.

St Thomas More (adapted)

A low prayer, a high prayer, I send through space. Arrange them thyself, O thou king of grace.

THE POEM-BOOK OF THE GAEL

Teach me your ways, O Lord; make them known to me. Teach me to live according to your truth.

PSALM 25:4–5

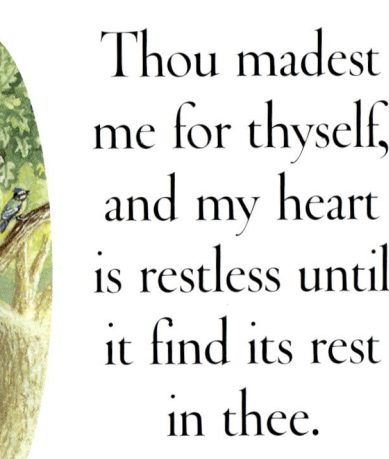

Thou madest me for thyself, and my heart is restless until it find its rest in thee.

St Augustine of Hippo

We can do
no great things,
only small things
with great love.

MOTHER TERESA OF CALCUTTA

Lord, grant that I may live to be Steadfast and patient as a tree,

With roots held firm while branches bend, Whate'er the trials on me descend.

DAVID GRAY

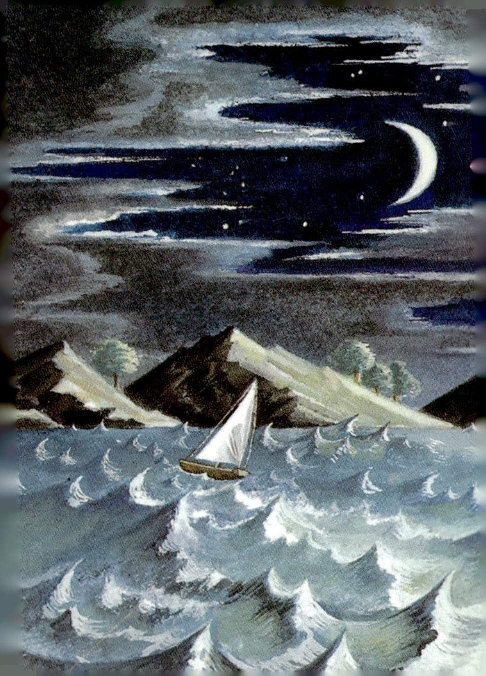

In the darkness

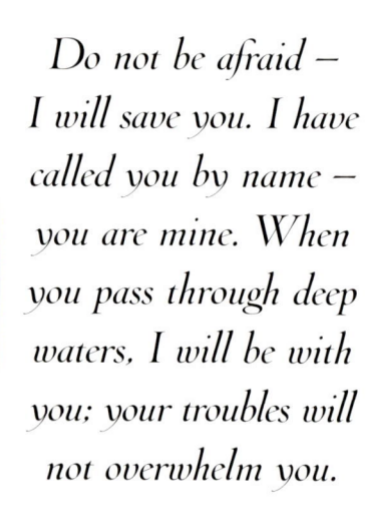

Do not be afraid — I will save you. I have called you by name — you are mine. When you pass through deep waters, I will be with you; your troubles will not overwhelm you.

Isaiah 43:1–2

In the
darkness,
hear my
prayer.

Lord, thou art life, though I be dead,
Love's fire thou art, however cold I be.

CHRISTINA ROSSETTI

Create in me
a pure heart,
O God; and
renew a steadfast
spirit within me.

PSALM 51:10

Lord Jesus Christ,
have mercy on me.

TRADITIONAL PRAYER

I'm tired, Lord, but I'll lift one foot if you'll lift the other for me.

Sadie Patterson

Dear God, be good to me. The sea is so wide and my boat is so small.

BRETON FISHERMAN'S PRAYER

In quietness and trust is your strength.

ISAIAH 30:15

As the rain hides the stars, as the clouds veil the blue of the sky, so the dark happenings of my lot hide the shining of your face from me.

Yet, if I may
hold your hand
in the darkness,
it is enough.

GAELIC PRAYER

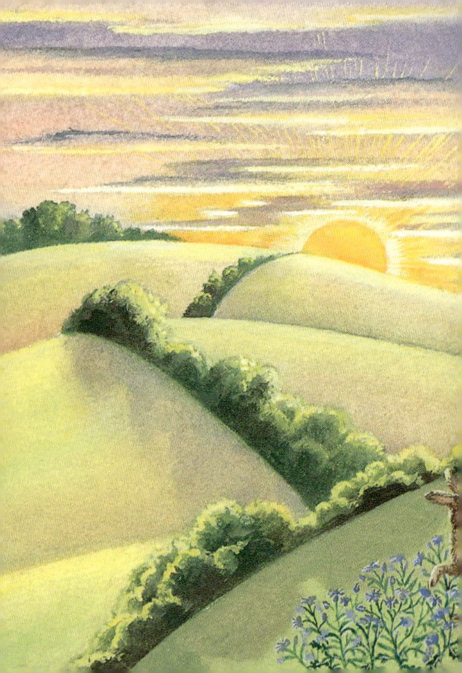

New every morning

Each and every morning, fresh as the dew, may your love come to me, making me new.

AUTHOR UNKNOWN

Now that daylight fills the sky, I lift my heart to God on high.

FIFTH-CENTURY HYMN

Lord, make me an instrument of your peace; where there is hatred, let me sow love;

where there is
injury, pardon;
where there is
discord, union;
where there is
doubt, faith;

where there is
despair, hope;
where there is
darkness, light;
where there is
sadness, joy.

ST FRANCIS OF ASSISI

Lord, make me like crystal that your light may shine through me.

KATHARINE MANSFIELD

Let this day,
O Lord, add some
knowledge or good
deed to yesterday.

LANCELOT ANDREWES

You, Lord,
give perfect peace
to those who keep
their purpose firm
and put their
trust in you.

Isaiah 26:3